3 3520 00066067 8

W9-BUU-661

DATE DUE

APR 12 2014	
JUN 30 2014	
AUG 18 2015	

BRODART, CO.   Cat. No. 23-221

AMAZING ORIGAMI

Origami Wild Animals

Lisa Miles

Gareth Stevens
Publishing

Please visit our website, www.garethstevens.com. For a free color catalog of all our high-quality books, call toll free 1-800-542-2595 or fax 1-877-542-2596.

Library of Congress Cataloging-in-Publication Data

Miles, Lisa.
   Origami wild animals / Lisa Miles.
      pages   cm. – (Amazing origami)
   Includes index.
   ISBN 978-1-4339-9665-8 (pbk.)
   ISBN 978-1-4339-9666-5 (6-pack)
   ISBN 978-1-4339-9664-1 (library binding)
   1. Origami–Juvenile literature. 2. Animals–Juvenile literature.   I. Title.
TT872.5.M559 2013
   736'.982–dc23

                                                          2012050332

First Edition

Published in 2014 by
Gareth Stevens Publishing
111 East 14th Street, Suite 349
New York, NY 10003

Copyright © 2014 Arcturus Publishing

Models and photography: Belinda Webster and Michael Wiles
Text: Lisa Miles
Design: Emma Randall
Editors: Anna Brett, Becca Clunes, and Joe Harris
Animal photography: Shutterstock

Printed in the United States of America

CPSIA compliance information: Batch #CS13GS: For further information contact Gareth Stevens, New York, New York at 1-800-542-2595.

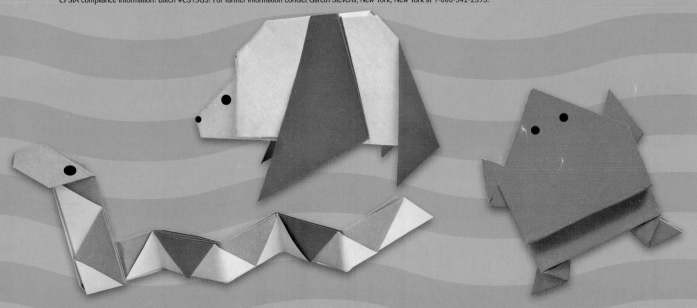

Contents

Basic Folds 4

Bases 6

Fox 8

Snake 12

Panda 16

Elephant 20

Giraffe 24

Frog..28

Glossary, Further Reading, and Index 32

Basic Folds

Origami has been popular in Japan for hundreds of years and is now loved all around the world. You can make great origami models with just one sheet of paper... and this book shows you how!

The paper used in origami is thin but strong, so that it can be folded many times. It is usually colored on one side. You can also use ordinary scrap paper, but make sure it's not too thick.

Origami models often share the same folds and basic designs, known as "bases." This introduction explains some of the folds and bases that you will need for the projects in this book. When making the models, follow the key below to find out what the lines and arrows mean. And always crease well!

KEY

valley fold - - - - - - - - - -
mountain fold ....

step fold (mountain and valley fold next to each other)

direction to move paper
push ◄

MOUNTAIN FOLD

To make a mountain fold, fold the paper so that the crease is pointing up toward you, like a mountain.

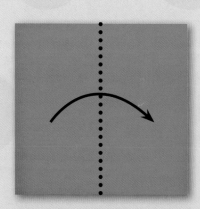 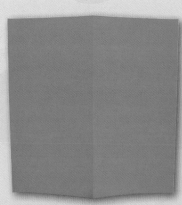

VALLEY FOLD

To make a valley fold, fold the paper the other way, so that the crease is pointing away from you, like a valley.

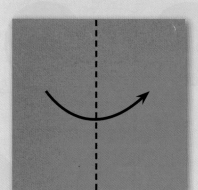 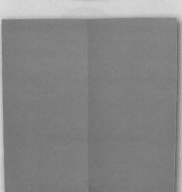

INSIDE REVERSE FOLD

An inside reverse fold is useful if you want to make a nose or a tail, or if you want to flatten off the shape of another part of an origami model.

① Practice by first folding a piece of paper diagonally in half. Make a valley fold on one point and crease.

② It's important to make sure that the paper is creased well. Run your finger over the crease two or three times.

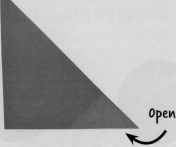

③ Unfold and open up the corner slightly. Refold the crease nearest to you into a mountain fold.

Open

④ Open up the paper a little more and then tuck the tip of the point inside. Close the paper. This is the view from the underside of the paper.

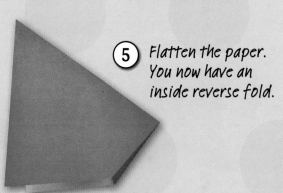

⑤ Flatten the paper. You now have an inside reverse fold.

OUTSIDE REVERSE FOLD

An outside reverse fold is useful if you want to make a head, beak, foot, or another part of your model that sticks out.

① Practice by first folding a piece of paper diagonally in half. Make a valley fold on one point and crease.

② It's important to make sure that the paper is creased well. Run your finger over the crease two or three times.

③ Unfold and open up the corner slightly. Refold the crease farthest away from you into a valley fold.

Open

④ Open up the paper a little more and start to turn the corner inside out. Then close the paper when the fold begins to turn.

⑤ You now have an outside reverse fold. You can either flatten the paper or leave it rounded out.

Bases

WATERBOMB BASE

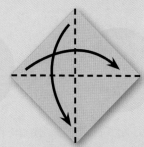

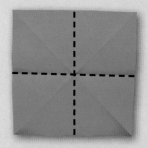

(1) Start with a square of paper, the point turned toward you. Make two diagonal valley folds.

(2) The paper should now look like this. Turn it over.

(3) Make two valley folds along the horizontal and vertical lines.

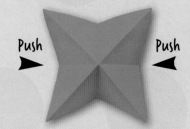

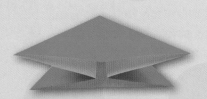

Push   Push

(4) Push the paper into this shape, so the center spot pops up.

(5) Push the sides in, bringing the back and front sections together.

(6) Flatten the paper. You now have a waterbomb base.

KITE BASE

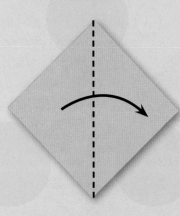

(1) Start with the point turned toward you. Valley fold it in half diagonally.

(2) Valley fold the left section to meet the center crease.

(3) Do the same on the other side.

(4) You now have a kite base.

BIRD BASE

1 Follow the first four steps of the Waterbomb base. The paper should look like this.

2 Hold the paper by opposite diagonal corners. Push the two corners together so that the shape begins to collapse. It should collapse into a square.

3 Turn the open end to face you. Then valley fold the top left flap to the center crease.

4 Do the same on the other side.

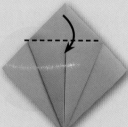

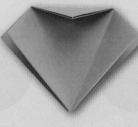

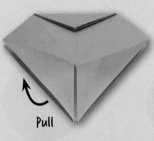

5 Valley fold the top triangle.

6 Unfold the top and sides and you have the shape shown here.

7 Take the bottom corner and begin to open out the upper flap by gently pulling upwards.

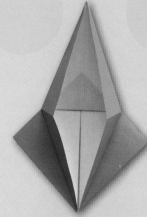

8 The paper should open like a bird's beak. Open out the flap as far as it will go.

9 Flatten the paper so that you now have this shape. Turn the paper over.

10 The paper should now look like this. Repeat steps 3 through 9 on this side.

11 You now have a bird base. The two flaps at the bottom are separated by an open slit.

Fox

In many traditional stories, the fox is a symbol of trickery and cunning. You'll find that making this origami fox isn't too tricky, though!

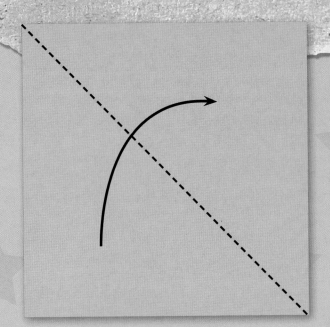

1 Start with a square of paper, colored side down. Valley fold in half diagonally.

2 Valley fold the bottom corner up.

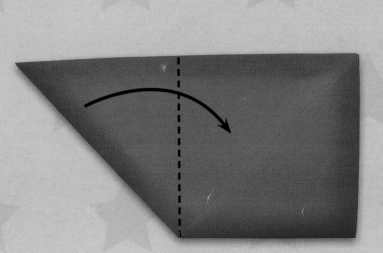

3 Now valley fold the left corner in to meet it.

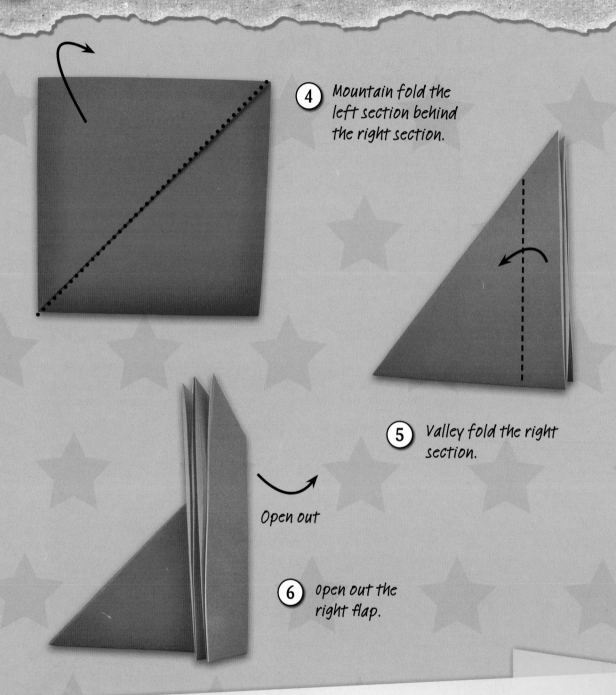

4 Mountain fold the left section behind the right section.

5 Valley fold the right section.

Open out

6 Open out the right flap.

Did You Know?

Foxes live underground in tunnels called dens. They sometimes share their dens with badgers!

Push

7 Push down the inside triangle to make a snout.

8 Valley fold the tail.

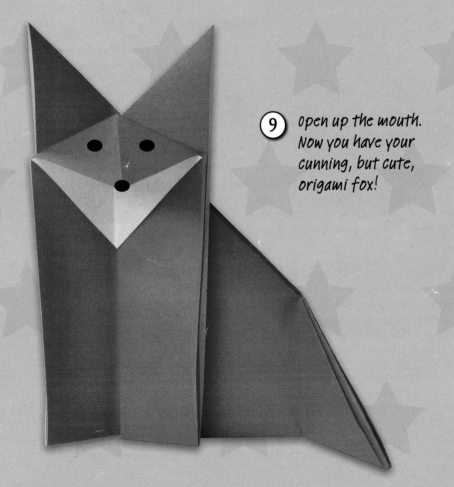

9 Open up the mouth. Now you have your cunning, but cute, origami fox!

Snake

Snakes don't have legs, so instead they use their long, muscular bodies to pull themselves along the ground in a wavy motion.

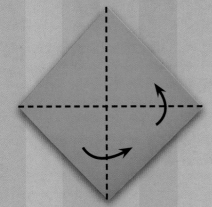

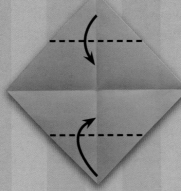

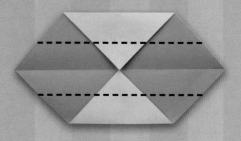

① Turn the paper with the point towards you. Make two diagonal valley folds.

② Valley fold the top and bottom corners to meet in the center.

③ Valley fold the top and bottom sections to meet in the center.

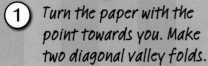

④ Repeat step 3.

⑤ The paper should now look like this.

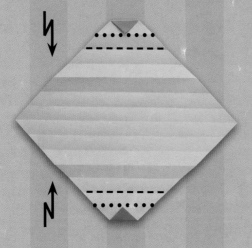

⑥ Unfold and turn the paper over. Then start to make a series of step folds inwards from both ends.

⑦ Continue to step fold. A pattern like this should appear.

Did You Know?

When snakes flick their tongues in and out, they are actually smelling the air.

(8) Repeat step 7.

(9) From the left, count in two and a half diamonds. Mountain fold the paper back on that line.

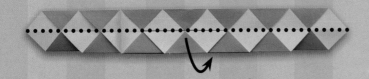

(10) Unfold the last fold you made. Now mountain fold the bottom section back behind the top section.

Use this crease

(11) Using the crease on the left that you made in step 9, make an outside reverse fold.

12 Mountain fold the top left corner.

13 Unfold, then make an outside reverse fold to create the snake's head.

14 Make alternate mountain and valley folds along the body.

15 Arrange the model like this. Now you have a zigzagging origami snake!

Panda

The panda is well known for its striking black-and-white markings. Origami paper that is dark on one side and white on the other works really well for this model.

Start with a waterbomb base

1 Find out how to make a waterbomb base on page 6. If you are using two-color paper, make the base with the white side facing out. Valley fold the right flap.

2 Do the same on the other side.

Open up

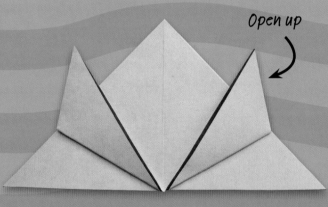

3 Gently open up the flap on the right.

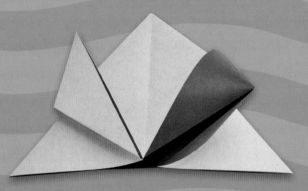

4 Make an outside reverse fold on this flap. Then do the same on the other side.

5 Valley fold the right tip of the bottom point.

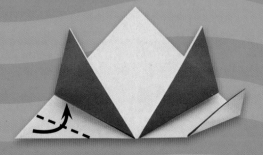

6 Do the same on the other side.

Did You Know?

Pandas have to eat a whole lot of bamboo!
They spend between 11 and 14 hours
every day foraging and eating.

Open up

7 Gently open up the
bottom right flap.

8 Make an outside reverse
fold. Then do the same on
the other side.

9 Mountain fold the paper in
half along the center crease.

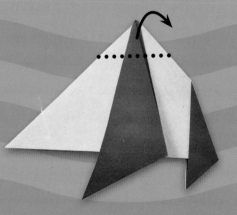

10 Turn the paper sideways, so that you now
have the shape of the panda's body and
legs. Mountain fold the top corner.

11 Unfold, then make an inside reverse fold to create the panda's back, as shown.

12 Step fold to make the panda's face.

13 Mountain fold the left point.

14 Unfold, then tuck the paper in to give the panda a blunt nose.

15 Open it out and stand it up to make a perfect origami panda!

Elephant

Medium

An elephant's trunk is strong and sensitive. An elephant uses it for grasping food and sucking up water. Here's how to make an origami elephant with an impressive trunk!

1. Find out how to make a kite base on page 6. Turn it upside down and turn the paper over.

2. Mountain fold the paper in half.

3. The paper should now look like this.

4. Open the paper out and then make a valley fold, to create a step fold as shown. Then turn the paper over.

5. Valley fold the bottom tip to meet the edge of the paper above.

6. The paper should now look like this.

Did You Know?

Elephants are very intelligent animals. Many scientists say that they are just as clever as gorillas and chimpanzees.

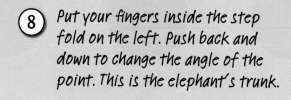

⑦ Turn the paper over. Mountain fold in half along the center crease so that the right side folds behind the left.

⑧ Put your fingers inside the step fold on the left. Push back and down to change the angle of the point. This is the elephant's trunk.

⑨ Flatten the paper. Valley fold the top point.

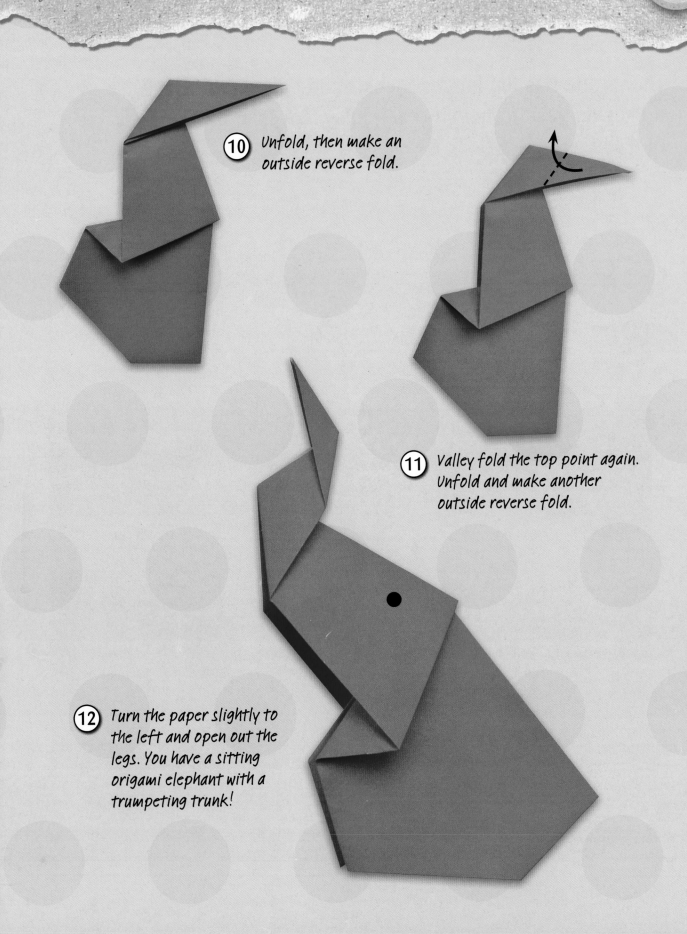

10 Unfold, then make an outside reverse fold.

11 Valley fold the top point again. Unfold and make another outside reverse fold.

12 Turn the paper slightly to the left and open out the legs. You have a sitting origami elephant with a trumpeting trunk!

Giraffe

The giraffe has the longest neck of any animal on Earth. It uses its neck to help it reach juicy leaves at the tops of trees.

Start with
a bird
base

1 Find out how to make a bird base on
page 7. Position it so that the flaps
with the open slit are on the left.

2 Take the right flap on the bottom
layer and swing it around behind
to the left, so that the two flaps
are now in the middle as shown.

Pull

Pull

3 Take the left and right points, one
in each hand, and gently pull the
base open, so that it looks like this.

4 Continue pulling gently until the middle
section starts to open like a bird's beak.

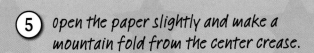

5 Open the paper slightly and make a
mountain fold from the center crease.

Did You Know?

Giraffes are normally 16 to 20 feet (5 to 6 m) tall.
That's taller than three average-sized humans standing
on each other's shoulders!

6 Close the paper again and press the left
and right points together to make a star.

7 Bring the bottom point up to meet
the top point. Flatten the paper.

8 Turn the paper over, so that
the point is now facing down.

9 Push the left point up and back
so that the back flap goes behind,
and the front flap swings around
in front.

Push ▶

10 Flatten the paper.
Valley fold the
right point.

11 Unfold, then make an outside reverse fold to create the giraffe's back legs.

12 Valley fold the top point.

13 Unfold, then do an outside reverse fold to create the giraffe's head.

14 Stand up your origami giraffe and show off that incredible neck!

Frog

Frogs move by jumping on their strong back legs. Here's how to make an origami frog that can spring into action!

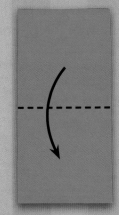

① Start with a square of paper, colored side down. Valley fold it in half from left to right.

② Valley fold it in half again by bringing the top section down.

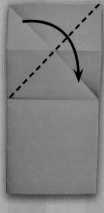

③ Valley fold the flap on the top layer to meet the top edge of the paper.

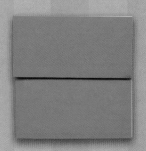

④ The paper should now look like this.

⑤ Unfold the last two steps. Valley fold the top right corner.

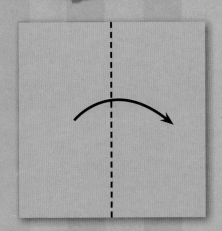

⑥ Unfold, then valley fold the top left corner.

⑦ The paper should now look like this.

⑧ Unfold the top section of the paper.

Did You Know?

Frogs are famously good at jumping. Some types of frogs can jump up to 50 times the length of their bodies!

Push

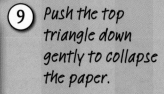

(9) Push the top triangle down gently to collapse the paper.

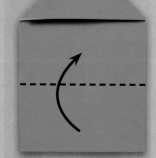

(10) Flatten down the paper at the top to make a triangle. Valley fold the bottom section to meet the edge of the triangle.

(11) Take the bottom flap on the right and valley fold it to meet the center, so that it sits beneath the triangle.

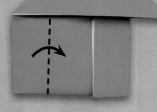

(12) Do the same on the other side.side.

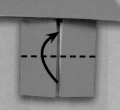

(13) Valley fold the bottom section to meet the edge of the triangle.

(14) Valley fold both bottom corners.

(15) Unfold the bottom sections. Poke in the top corners to make a boat shape, as shown in step 16.

16) Flatten the paper. Valley fold the bottom right corner. Do the same on the other side.

17) Valley fold the bottom right corner again, the other way. Do the same on the other side.

18) Now valley fold the top right corner. Do the same on the other side.

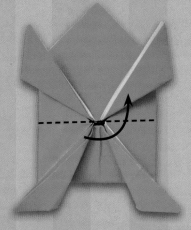

20) Valley fold the top section down. The fold is very tight!

21) The paper should now look like this.

19) Valley fold the paper in half along the center crease.

22) Turn the paper over and you have an origami frog. Push your finger down on the fold at the back to see it jump!

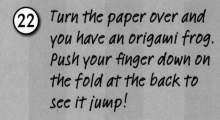

Glossary

bamboo A tall and fast-growing plant found in tropical countries. The woody, hollow stems of bamboo plants are used to make objects such as furniture.

base A simple, folded shape that is used as the starting point for many different origami projects.

crease A line in a piece of paper made by folding.

forage To search for food.

grasp To hold onto something tightly.

marking A pattern on an animal's fur.

mountain fold An origami step where a piece of paper is folded so that the crease is pointing upwards, like a mountain.

muscular With big, strong muscles.

step fold A mountain fold and valley fold next to each other.

trickery The act of playing tricks on people.

valley fold An origami step where a piece of paper is folded so that the crease is pointing downwards, like a valley.

waterbomb A traditional origami shape, which can be filled with water.

Further Reading

Robinson, Nick. *Absolute Beginner's Origami.* New York: Potter Craft, 2006.
Robinson, Nick. *World's Best Origami.* New York: Alpha Books, 2010.
Van Sicklen, Margaret. *Origami on the Go: 40 Paper-Folding Projects for Kids Who Love to Travel.* New York: Workman Publishing Company, 2009.

Index

B
badgers 10
bamboo 18
bird bases 7, 25
C
chimpanzees 22
D
dens 10
E
elephants 20–23

F
foxes 8–11
frogs 28–31
G
giraffes 24–27
gorillas 22
I
intelligence 22
J
jumping 28, 30, 31

K
kite bases 6, 21
L
legs 12, 18, 23, 27, 28
M
markings 16
N
necks 24, 27
P
pandas 16–19

S
snakes 12–15
T
tails 5, 11
tongues 14
trees 24
trunks 20, 22, 23
W
water 20
waterbomb bases 6, 17